Struggling
with Scripture

Struggling
with Scripture

Walter Brueggemann
William C. Placher
Brian K. Blount

Westminster John Knox Press
LOUISVILLE • LONDON

The essays in this book were originally presented on November 3 and 4, 2000, at East Liberty Presbyterian Church, in Pittsburgh, Pa., as part of a conference titled Biblical Authority and the Church, sponsored by the Covenant Network of Presbyterians.

Book design by Sharon Adams
Cover design by Pam Poll Graphic Design

First edition
Published by Westminster John Knox Press
Louisville, Kentucky

This book is printed on acid-free paper that meets the American National Standards Institute Z39.48 standard. ∞

PRINTED IN THE UNITED STATES OF AMERICA

Library of Congress Cataloging-in-Publication Data
Brueggemann, Walter.
    Struggling with scripture / Walter Brueggemann, William C. Placher, Brian K. Blount.
        p. cm.
    ISBN 0-664-22485-7 (alk. paper)
    1. Bible—Evidences, authority, etc. I. Placher, William C. (William Carl), 1948– II. Blount, Brian K., 1955– III. Title.

BS480 .B74 2001
220.1'3—dc21   2001046838

Contents

Struggling
with Scripture

Introduction

An educated guess tells me that the reader of this page is highly intelligent, a member of a mainline church who has certain unresolved reservations about the Bible and perhaps a sneaking suspicion that people who read it more literally take it more seriously.

Whether or not the description fits, you have in your hands a truly fine book. Its three authors, every one a biblical scholar, have wisdom and wit, and take Scripture with utter seriousness, the more so by not confusing biblical authority with biblical infallibility.

Professor Blount recalls a line from the movie *A League of Our Own*. When one of the players complains that playing baseball is too hard, the coach, played by Tom Hanks, answers her, "It's baseball. It's supposed to be hard. If it weren't hard, then everyone would do it." Adds Blount, Christian faith and the biblical interpretation that goes along with it are also hard. "Not everyone can do it, not everyone wants to do it."

I was reminded of his last point recently when I pulled up behind a car with a bumper sticker that read, "God said it, I believe it, that settles it."

But the Bible is neither self-evident nor self-interpreting. It is a sacred book—that goes without saying; after all, it is the founding document of every Christian church in the world. But, sacred in status, is it also sacred in origin? Is it the Word of God or, rather, incredibly inspired words about God? Does it tell us how God sees things or how Jeremiah and St. Paul saw them? These questions, I think,

1

demand "either-or" answers, because to say that parts of the Bible are divine while other parts are human leads quickly to a welter of confusion.

If we conclude that the Bible is a human product, we are by no means denying the reality of God. Rather, we are simply admitting that there is no escaping our personal and cultural history, nor the personal and cultural history of all writers, no matter what their subject matter. Professor Placher asks how we draw the line "between the cultural assumptions in which the message of the Bible is presented and the message which is presented in them." He recognizes that in biblical times slavery was a given, women were devalued, rulers were generally revered, and homosexuality denounced. But in our quite different culture, slavery is denounced, as are many rulers, and women and gay people are fighting for what Christians, Jews, and Muslims among them consider their God-given rights.

And what of religious pluralism, today a very present fact of life the world around? Should we show empathetic awareness of other faiths or make exclusivistic claims for one religious tradition only, which somehow always happens to be our own?

Last, there is the matter of individual interpretation. Professor Brueggemann recalls a dispute in Israel as to whom the religious Jew really is—Orthodox, Conservative, or Reformed. He reports an Israeli journalist's conclusion: "If any Jew wins, all Jews lose." Couldn't the same be said of Presbyterians, of Lutherans or Roman Catholics, of biblical and U.S. Constitutional scholars? "If anyone wins, all lose." In praise of interpretation, Professor Brueggemann calls it "a God-given resistance to monologue."

I suggested at the outset that highly intelligent people often have reservations about the Bible. Without question, honest uncertainty beats hard-nosed certitude. But it is a mistake to be paralyzed by uncertainty, especially when life so frequently calls upon us to act wholeheartedly without absolute certainty. Moreover, wrestling with Scripture, far from a sign of weakness, is a reflection of religious faithfulness. What else should you wrestle with if not the Bible? What struggle offers more reward? The Bible is like a sacrament, a means of grace; it mediates God's presence in the life of each of us and God's concern for the whole planet. Preaching from its pages for over forty years, I have encountered a God who bruises our egos but mends our hearts; a God who pleads without ceasing the cause of the poor and needy, who implores us to revere, not ravish the earth, and to stay on the stony, long, and ofttimes lonely road that leads to world peace.

I am sure readers will feel as I do—grateful to professors Brueggemann, Placher, and Blount for the pleasure and profit their scholarship, wisdom, and wit bring all of us in *Struggling with Scripture*.

William Sloane Coffin

Biblical Authority:
A Personal Reflection

Walter Brueggemann

Professor of Old Testament
Columbia Theological Seminary

T he issue of the authority of the Bible is a perennial and urgent one for those of us who claim and intend to stake our lives on its attestation. But for all of the perennial and urgent qualities of the question, the issue of biblical authority is bound, in any case, to remain endlessly unsettled and therefore, I believe, perpetually disputatious. It cannot be otherwise, and so we need not hope for a "settlement" of the issue. The unsettling and disputatious quality of the question is, I believe, given in the text itself, because the Bible is ever so endlessly "strange and new."[1] It always, inescapably, outdistances our categories of understanding and explanation, of interpretation and control. Because the Bible is, as we confess, "the live word of the living God," it will not submit in any compliant way to the accounts we prefer to give of it. There is something intrinsically unfamiliar about the book, and when we seek to override that unfamiliarity we are on the hazardous ground of idolatry.

Because I am not well schooled in the long, formal discussions and considerations concerning "the authority of

Scripture" (perhaps better left to theologians), I offer here a quite personal reflection on the authority of Scripture, to consider how it is that I work with, relate to, and submit to the Bible. I do not suggest that my way is in any sense commendable or normative. Nor do I know if my ruminations will particularly serve the current crisis in the church, and I do not intend my statement to be particularly attentive to the "culture wars" in which we are engaged.

Thus I offer a more or less innocent personal account, though of course none of our personal accounts is very innocent. Your invitation has provided an opportunity for me to think clearly about my own practice. In the process, moreover, I have become convinced that we will be well served if we can be in some way honest about the intimate foundations of our personal stance on these questions. Indeed, rather than loud, settled slogans about the Bible, we might do better to consider the odd and intimate ways in which we have each, alike and differently, been led to where we are about the Bible. In setting out such a statement, I say at the outset that you do me a great privilege by inviting me here, a non-Presbyterian, though I hope when I have finished you will judge me to be reliably, if not with excessive intensity, Reformed.

I begin by telling you about what I take to be the defining moment in my attachment to the Bible. In my German Evangelical upbringing, confirmation was a very big deal. In that act of confirmation, the pastor (in my case, my father) selected a "confirmation verse" for each confirmand, a verse to mark one's life—read while hands were laid on in confirmation, read at one's funeral, and read many times in between. My father, on that occasion of confirmation, read over me Psalm 119:105:

> Your word is a lamp to my feet
> and a light to my path.

He did, in that act, more than he knew. Providentially, I have no doubt, he marked my life by this book that would be lamp and light, to illumine a way to obedience, to mark a way to fullness, joy, and well-being. The more I reflect on that moment, the more I am sure that I have been bound more than I knew to this book.

Before that moment of confirmation in baptismal vows, in my nurture in the church, my church prepared me to attend to the Bible in a certain way. I am a child of the Prussian Union, a church body created in 1817, on the 300th anniversary of Luther's theses. The Prussian king was weary of Calvinists and Lutherans arguing about the Eucharist and so decreed an ecumenical church that was in its very founding to be ecumenical and not confessional, open to diversity, and aimed not at any agreement beyond a broad consensus of evangelical faith that intended to protect liberty of conscience. This is the church body that brought to the United States a deep German church slogan now taken over and claimed by many others:

> In essentials unity;
> in nonessentials liberty;
> in all things charity.[2]

In actuality, moreover, the last line, "in all things charity," became the working interpretive principle that produced a fundamentally irenic church.

The pastoral ambiance of that climate for Bible reading may be indicated by two examples. First, the quarrels over historical-critical reading of the Bible, faced by every church soon or late, were firmly settled as long ago as 1870, when one seminary teacher was forced out of teaching but quickly restored to a pastoral position of esteem, so the issue did not again cause trouble. Second, in its only seminary, Eden Seminary, there was no systematic theologian on the faculty until 1946, and things were managed well enough in a mood of trustful piety that produced not hardnosed certitude, but rather an irenic charity of liberated generosity. All of that was before my moment of confirmation, in which I became an heir to that tradition, with its trustful engagement with the book as "lamp" and "light."

After my confirmation came a series of teachers who shaped me in faith, after my father, my first and best teacher, who taught me the artistry as well as the authority of Scripture. In college my first Bible teacher was a beloved man still at work in the church, still my friend. He mostly confused me about JEDP, perhaps because he did not understand very well himself, being a theologian and not an exegete.

In seminary I had an astonishing gift of Bible teachers, none of whom published, as perhaps the best teachers do not. Allen Wehrli had studied under Hermann Gunkel in Halle and taught us the vast density of artistry of the Bible, with attention to the form of the text. His pedagogy, for which he was renowned in our circle, was imaginative storytelling; he understood that the Bible is narrative, long before G. Ernest Wright or Fred Craddock. Lionel Whiston introduced us in 1959 to the first traces of Gerhard von Rad that reached English readers. Von Rad showed that the practice of biblical faith is first of all recital, and I have devoured his work ever since.[3] I learned from Wehrli and Whiston that the Bible is essentially an open, artistic, imaginative narrative of God's staggering care for the world, a narrative that will feed and nurture into obedience, that builds community precisely by respect for the liberty of the Christian man or woman.[4]

After seminary, purely by accident, at Union Seminary in New York, I stumbled on to James Muilenburg (arguably the most compelling Old Testament teacher of his generation), who taught us that the Bible will have its authoritative, noncoercive way if we but attend with educated alertness to the cadences and sounds of the text as given in all its detail. And, since graduate school, I have been blessed by a continuing host of insistent teachers—seminarians who would not settle easily, church people who asked new and probing questions—and I have even read other Bible teachers, to mixed advantage. But mostly my continuing education has been from the writing and witness of people whose faith is powered by the text to live lives of courage, suffering, and sacrifice. In noncoercive ways and seemingly without effort at forcing anyone else, they have found this book a wind and source and energy for the fullness of the true life lived unafraid.

When I think about that moment of confirmation in 1947, seeing it better now than I did then, I have come to see that gathered all that day was my church tradition of simple, irenic piety from the past, and gathered all that day was this succession of teachers still to come who would let me see how broad and deep and demanding and generous is this text, how utterly beyond me in its richness, and yet, held concretely in my hands, offering to me and to those around me unprecedented generativity. "A lamp to my feet and a light to my path." How remarkable a gift that my father knew all that and willed all of that and gathered all of that for me on that incidental day in 1947 at St. Paul's Church in Saline County.

I take so much time with my particular history not because you are concerned with it, or because the story has any great merit, but perhaps as nothing more than the pondering of an aging Bible man. I tell you in order to attest that how we read the Bible, each of us, is partly a plot of family, neighbors, and friends (a socialization process) and partly the God-given accident of long-term development in faith. From that come two learnings.

1. The real issues of biblical authority and interpretation are not likely to be settled by erudite cognitive formulation or by appeal to classic settlements, but live beneath such contention in often unrecognized and uncriticized ways that are deeply powerful, especially if rooted (as they may be for most of us) amid hurt, anger, or anxiety.

2. Real decisions about biblical meanings are mostly not decided on the spot but are long-term growths of habit and conviction that emerge, function, and shape, often long before they are recognized. And if that is so, then the disputes require not frontal arguments that are mostly exercises in self-entertainment but long-term pastoral attentiveness to each other in good faith.

If that is true, a church in dispute will require great self-knowing candor and a generous openness to allow the legitimacy of long-term nurture that gifts others. Such attentiveness may be so generous as to entertain the thought that the story of someone else's long-term nurture could be a gift not only for that person but could be, once removed, a transformative gift to me when I read the text through their nurture that is marked, as are we all, by joy, doubt, fear, and hurt.

With this perhaps too long personal reflection, I will now identify six facets of biblical interpretation about which I know something that I believe is likely to be operative among us all.

Inherency

The Bible is inherently the live Word of God that addresses us concerning the character and will of the gospel-giving God, empowering us to an alternative life in the world. I say "inherently" because we can affirm that it is in itself intrinsically so. While I give great credence to "reader response" (how can one not?) and while I believe in the indeterminacy of the text to some large extent, finally the Bible is forceful and consistent in its main theological claim. That claim concerns the conviction that the God who creates the world in love redeems the world in suffering and will consummate the world in joyous well-being. That flow of conviction about the self-disclosure of God in the Bible is surely the main claim of apostolic faith upon which the church is fundamentally agreed. That fundamental agreement about main claims is, of course, the beginning of the conversation and not its conclusion, but it is a deep and important beginning point for which I use the term *inherent*.

From that four things follow:

1. Because this is the foundation of apostolic faith to which we all give attestation, it means that all of us in the church are bound together, as my tradition affirms, "in essentials unity." It also means, moreover, that in disputes about biblical authority nobody has high ground morally or hermeneutically. We share a common commitment about the truth of the book that makes us equal before the book as it does around the table.

2. The inherency of evangelical truth in the Bible is focused on its main claims. From that it follows that there

is much in the text that is "lesser," not a main claim, but a lesser voice that probes and attempts, over the generations, to carry the main claims to specificity, characteristically informed by particular circumstance and characteristically in the text open to variation, nuance, and even contradiction. It is a primal Reformation principle, given main claims and lesser voices in the text, that our faith is evangelical, linked to the news and not biblicism, thus recognizing the potential tension or distinction between good news and lesser claims. That particular tension and distinction is, of course, the arena of much dispute in the church just now, and it is important at the outset to make the distinction, so that we can see the true subject of the dispute.

3. The inherent Word of God in the biblical text is, of course, refracted through many authors who were not disembodied voices of revealed truth. They were, rather, circumstance-situated men and women of faith (as are we all) who said what their circumstance permitted and required them to speak, as they were able, of that which is truly inherent. It is this human refraction, of course, that makes inescapable the hard work of critical study, so that every text is invited to a suspicious scrutiny whereby we may consider the ways in which bodied humanness has succeeded or not succeeded in being truthful and faithful witness. Each of us, moreover, would concede that some bodied human witnesses in the text succeeded more effectively than some others.

4. Given both inherency and circumstance-situated human refraction, the Bible is endlessly a surprise beyond us that Karl Barth famously and rightly termed "strange and new." The Bible is not a fixed, frozen, readily exhausted read; it is rather a "script," always reread, through which the Spirit makes new. When the church adjudicates the

inherent and the circumstance-situated, the church of whatever ilk is sore tempted to settle, close, and idolize. And therefore inherency of an evangelical kind demands a constant resistance to familiarity. Nobody makes the final read; nobody's read is final or inerrant, precisely because the Key Character in the book who creates, redeems, and consummates is always beyond us in holy hiddenness.[5] When we push boldly through the hiddenness, wanting to know more clearly, what we thought was holy ground turns out to be a playground for idolatry. Our reading of inherency, then, is inescapably provisional reading. It is rightly done with the modesty that belongs to those who are yet to be surprised always again by what is "strange and new."

Interpretation

The claim of biblical authority is not difficult as it pertains to the main affirmations of apostolic faith. But from that base line, the hard, disputatious work is interpretation that needs to be recognized precisely for what it is: nothing other than interpretation. The Bible, our mothers and fathers have always known, is not self-evident and self-interpreting, and the Reformers did not mean that at all when they escaped the church's magisterium.[6] Rather, the Bible requires and insists upon human interpretation that is inescapably subjective, necessarily provisional, and, as you are living witnesses, inevitably disputatious.

I propose as an interpretive rule that all of our subjective, provisional, disputatious interpretation be taken, at the most, with quite tentative authority, in order that we may (1) make our best, most insistent claims, but then, with some regularity, we may (2) relinquish our pet interpretations and, together with our partners in dispute, fall back in joy into the inherent apostolic claims that outdistance all our too familiar and too partisan interpretations. We may learn from the rabbis the marvelous rhythm of deep interpretive dispute and profound common yielding in joy and affectionate well-being.[7] The sometimes characteristic and demonic mode of Reformed interpretation is not tentativeness and relinquishment but tentativeness that is readily hardened into absoluteness, whether of the right or of the left, of exclusive or of inclusive, a sleight-of-hand act of substituting our interpretive preference for the inherency of apostolic claims.

The process of interpretation that precludes final settlement on almost all questions is self-evident in the Bible itself. As Gerhard von Rad spent his life making clear, Deuteronomy is the model and engine of an ongoing interpretive dynamic in the Old Testament. Moses becomes the cipher for all those interpreters yet to come who dispute with the text of Moses, so that what we have in the text is Moses contra Moses.[8] We can see this dynamic in the text itself, for even Deuteronomy acknowledges that its own tradition is not from Sinai but is a derivative form and an extrapolation as a "second" (*deuteros*) reading for a new time and place (Deut. 17:18). Thus Moses enunciates the required interpretive principle:

> Not with our ancestors did the LORD make this covenant, but with us, who are all of us here alive today. (Deut. 5:3)

After the reiterated Decalogue of chapter 5, the tradition of Deuteronomy proceeds to extrapolate from Sinai for many chapters at the Jordan for a new circumstance. A stunning case in point is the Mosaic teaching in Deuteronomy 23:1–8 that bans from the community all those with distorted sexuality and all those who are foreigners. In Isaiah 56:3–8, this Mosaic teaching is frontally overturned in the Bible itself, offering what Herbert Donner terms an intentional "abrogation" of Mosaic law in new teaching.[9] The old, no doubt circumstance-driven exclusion in the mouth of Moses in Deuteronomy 23 is answered by a circumstance-driven inclusiveness in Isaiah 56.

To cite another example, in Deuteronomy 24:1–5, Moses teaches that marriages broken in infidelity cannot be restored, even if both parties want to get back together. But in Jeremiah 3, in a shocking reversal given in a pathos-filled poem, God's own voice indicates a readiness to violate that Torah teaching for the sake of restored marriage to Israel.[10] The old teaching is seen to be problematic even for God. The later text shows God prepared to move beyond the old prohibition in order that the inherent evangelical claims of God's graciousness may be fully available even to recalcitrant Israel. In at least embarrassment and perhaps in humiliation, the God of the poem in Jeremiah willfully overrides the old text in new circumstance of pathos. It becomes clear that the interpretive project that constitutes the final form of the text is itself profoundly polyvalent, yielding no single exegetical outcome, but allowing layers and layers of fresh reading in which God's own life and character are deeply engaged and put at risk.

As we observe the open dynamic of interpretation in the text itself, moreover, we ourselves are able to see that same dynamic operative in our own time and place. It is self-evident that new circumstances of reading permit us to see what we have not seen in the text heretofore. A clear case in point is that the ecological crisis now evokes awareness on our part that the Bible does indeed address the issues of a distorted, polluted creation, though in past "faithful" reading we missed all of that because we read in a specific time and place.[11] Interpretive humility invites us to recognize that reading in a particular time, place, and circumstance can never be absolute but is more than likely to be displaced by yet another reading in another time and place, a reading that may depart from or even judge the older reading or even the older text, as in these two cases from Deuteronomy.

The Spirit meets us always afresh in our faithful reading, in each new time, place, and circumstance. Anyone who imagines that reading is settled and eternal simply does not pay attention to the process in which we are all engaged, liberals and conservatives. Following George Steiner, I suspect that interpretation—albeit subjective, provisional, and disputatious—is a God-given resistance to monologue.[12] There is not one voice in Scripture, and to give any one voice in Scripture or in tradition authority to silence other voices surely distorts the text and misconstrues the liveliness that the text itself engenders in the interpretive community.

Imagination

Responsible interpretation requires and inevitably engages in imagination. Imagination makes us serious Calvinists nervous, because it smacks of subjective freedom to carry the text in undeveloped directions and to engage in fantasy. Apart from such a fear, I would insist that (1) imagination is in any case inevitable in the interpretive process if it is ever anything more than simple reiteration and that (2) faithful imagination is characteristically not autonomous fantasy but good-faith extrapolation.

I understand imagination to be the capacity to entertain images of meaning and reality that are out beyond the evident givens of observable experience.[13] That is, imagination is the hosting of "otherwise," and I submit that every serious teacher or preacher invites to "otherwise" beyond the evident givens, or we have nothing to say.[14] When we do such hosting of "otherwise," however, we must, of course, take risks and act daringly to push beyond what is known to that which is hoped and trusted but not yet in hand.

Interpretation is not the reiteration of the text. It is rather the movement of the text beyond itself in fresh ways, often ways never offered until this moment of utterance. A primal example, of course, is constituted by Jesus' parables, which open the listening community to possible futures.[15] Beyond parabolic teaching, however, there was in ancient Israel and in the early church observed wonder.[16] As eyewitnesses created texts out of observed and remembered miracles, there is no doubt that these texted miracles in turn became materials for imagination that pushed well beyond what is given or intended even in the text. This is an inescapable process for those of us who insist that this old text is a contemporary word to us. We transport ourselves out of the twenty-first century back to that ancient world or, conversely, we transpose ancient voices into contemporary voices of authority. We do it all the time:

> Those of us who think critically do not believe that the Old Testament was talking about Jesus, and yet we make the linkages.

> Surely Paul was not thinking of the crisis of sixteenth-century indulgences when he wrote about "faith alone."

> Surely Isaiah was not thinking, in writing Isaiah 65, of Martin Luther King Jr. having a dream of a new earth.

We make such leaps all the time:

> What a huge leap to imagine that the primal commission to "till" and "keep" the earth (Gen. 2:15) is really about environmental issues and the chemicals used by Iowa farmers. But we do it.
>
> What a huge leap to imagine that the ancient provision for jubilee in Leviticus 25 in fact concerns cancellation of third-world debts, with an implied critique of global capitalism. But we do it.
>
> What a huge leap to imagine that an ancient purity code in Leviticus 18 bears upon consenting gays and lesbians in the twenty-first century and is concerned with ordination. But we do it.

We do it, and we are commonly, all of us, committed to the high practice of subjective extrapolations, because we commonly have figured out that a cold, reiterative objectivity has no missional energy or moral force. We do it, and we will not stop doing it. But it is surely healing and humbling for us, all of us, to be self-knowing enough to concede that what we are doing in imaginative interpretation is not "inherent" but is subjective extrapolation that will not carry the freight of absoluteness.

No doubt Karl Barth, that great father of us all, understood this when he imagined for an instant that Romans 13 pertained to Christian obedience in Communist Hungary. Indeed, of imagination Barth himself could write:

> We must dismiss and resist to the very last any idea of the inferiority or untrustworthiness or even worth-

lessness of a "non-historical" depiction and narration of history. This is in fact only a ridiculous and middle-class habit of the modern Western mind which is supremely phantastic in its chronic lack of imaginative phantasy, and hopes to rid itself of its complexes through suppression. This habit has really no claim to the dignity and validity which it pretends. . . . But human possibility of knowing is not exhausted by the ability to perceive and comprehend. Imagination, too, belongs no less legitimately in its way to the human possibility of knowing. A man without imagination is more of an invalid than one who lacks a leg. But fortunately each of us is gifted somewhere and somehow with imagination, however starved this gift may be in some or misused by others.[17]

If we grant that interpretation is our bounden duty, then it follows, inescapably, I believe, that imagination is the vehicle for interpretation. This is what Moses was doing at the Jordan in Deuteronomy; this is what Jesus was doing in his rabbinic way, "You have heard it said of old." And this is what the church always does when it risks moving the text to its own time and place. Imagination can indeed be a gift of the Spirit, but it is a gift used with immense subjective freedom, which we would do better to concede even if that concession makes unmistakably clear that our imaginative interpretations cannot claim the shrillness of certainty but only the tentativeness of our best extrapolations. After our imaginative interpretations are made with vigor in dispute with others in the church, I submit that we must regularly, gracefully, and with modesty fall back from our best extrapolations to the sure apostolic claims that lie behind our extremities of imagination, liberal or conservative.

Ideology

A consideration of ideology is difficult among us, precisely because U.S. church people are largely innocent about our own interpretive work, and not often aware of or honest about the ways in which our own work is shot through with distorting vested interest.[18] But it is so, even if we are innocent about it. There is no interpretation of Scripture (or interpretation of anything else, for that matter) that is unaffected by the passions, convictions, and perceptions of the interpreter. Ideology is the self-deceiving practice of taking a part for the whole, of taking "my truth" for *the* truth, of running truth through a prism of the particular and palming off the particular as a universal.[19] It is so already in the text of Scripture itself, as current scholarship makes clear, because the Spirit-given text is given us by and through human authors.[20] It is so because Spirit-filled interpretation is given us by and through bodied authors who must make their way in the world, and in making our way, we do not see so clearly or love so dearly or follow so nearly as we might imagine.

There are endless examples of ideology at work in interpretation:

> The practice of historical criticism is no innocent practice, for it intends to fend off church authority and protect freedom for the autonomous interpreter.

> The practice of so-called canonical criticism is no innocent practice, for it intends to maintain old coherences of truth against the perceived threat of more recent fragmentation.

> The practice of high moralism is no innocent practice, even if it sounds disciplined and noble, for much of that high-grounded moralism comes from fear and is a strategy to fend off anxiety.

> The practice of communitarian inclusiveness is an interpretive posture that is no innocent practice, because it reflects a reaction against exclusivism and so is readily given to a kind of reactive carelessness.

There is enough of truth in every such interpretive posture and strategy—historical criticism, canonism, moralism, communitarianism, and a hundred others we might name—to make the posture credible and to gather a mass of constituency in order to maintain a sustained voice. But it is not, for reasons of ideology, innocent, and if not innocent, then it has no absolute claim.

In a disputatious church, a healthy practice might be to reflect upon the ideological passion, not of others, but of self and cohorts who agree. I believe that such reflection would invariably indicate:[21]

> That every passionate interpretive voice is shot through with vested interest, sometimes barely hidden, so shot through that it is completely predictable that interpreters who are restrictive about gays and lesbians will characteristically advocate high capitalism and a strong national defense; conversely, those who are "open and affirming" will characteristically maintain a critique of consumer capitalism and a whole cluster of issues along with it. One can argue in each case, of course, that such a package is only a theological-ethical coherence. Perhaps, but in no case, I should argue, is the package innocent, precisely because given the package, we incline to make the next decision without any critical reflection but only in order to sustain the package.

> That every vested interest has working in it, if it is passionate, a high measure of anxiety about deep

threats, perhaps perceived, perhaps imagined, and anxiety has a forceful passion to it that permits us to deal in wholesale categories without the nuance of the particular.[22] A judgment grounded in anxiety, anywhere on the theological spectrum, wants not to be disturbed or informed by the detail of facts on the ground.

That every vested interest shaped by anxiety has near its source old fears that are deep and hidden, but for all of that authoritative.

That every vested interest informed by anxiety and infused with fear has at its very bottom hurt, old hurt, new hurt, hurt for ourselves, for those remembered, for those we love; the pain, lingering, unhealed pain, becomes a hermeneutical principle out of which we will not be talked.

We can see such ideology in the text itself that surely reflects vested interest, anxiety, fear, and hurt. In Deuteronomy, as Carolyn Pressler has shown, the marriage laws are deeply patriarchal, perhaps echoed in some corrected form by Paul.[23] We can see it in Hananiah, who picked up the buoyant Zionism of Isaiah and, a century later, against Jeremiah turned it into an absolute principle that blinded him to lived reality.[24] We can see it in Ezra, who not only fathered Judaism but fended off other Judaisms in an exercise of complete domination and hegemony.

Every such ideological passion, liberal or conservative, may be encased in Scripture itself or enshrined in longstanding interpretation until it is absolute and trusted as decisive authority. And where ideology becomes loud and destructive in the interpretive community, we may be sure that the doses of anxiety, fear, and hurt within it are huge and finally irrepressible.

I am not suggesting that no distinctions can be made or

that it is so dark that all cats are gray. And certainly, given our ideological passions, we must go on and interpret in any case. But I do say that in our best judgments concerning Scripture, we might be aware enough of our propensity to distort in the service of vested interest, anxiety, fear, and hurt that we would recognize that our best interpretation might be not only vehicle but also block and distortion of the crucified truth of the gospel. If interpretation is unavoidable, as I think it is, whereby old text is made new, and if imagination is an inescapable practice, as it surely is, it is clear that interpretation and imagination are immensely open to traffic in our penultimate passions that seem to us so ultimate.

I have come belatedly to see, in my own case, that my hermeneutical passion is largely propelled by the fact that my father was a pastor economically abused by the church he served, economically abused as a means of control. I cannot measure the ways in which that felt awareness determines how I work, how I interpret, whom I read, whom I trust as a reliable voice. The wound is deep enough to pervade everything; I suspect, moreover, that I am not the only one. It could be that we turn our anxieties, fears, and hurts to good advantage as vehicles for obedience. But even in so doing, we are put on notice. We cannot escape, I believe, from such passions, but we can submit them to brothers and sisters whose own history of distortion is very different from our own and as powerful in its defining force.

Inspiration

It is traditional to speak of Scripture as "inspired." There is a long history of unhelpful formulations of what that notion might mean. Without appealing to classical attempts at formulation that characteristically have more to do with "testing" the Spirit (1 John 4:1) than with "not quenching" the Spirit (1 Thess. 5:19), we may affirm that the force of God's purpose, will, and capacity for liberation, reconciliation, and new life is everywhere around this text. In such an affirmation, of course, we say more than we can understand, for the claim is precisely an acknowledgment that in and through this text, God's wind blows through and blows past all our critical and confessional categories of reading and understanding. That blowing force that powers and enlivens, moreover, pertains not simply to the origin of the text but to its transmission and interpretation among us. The Spirit will not be regimented, and therefore none of our reading is guaranteed to be inspired. But it does happen—on occasion.

It does happen that we are blown in and through the text beyond ourselves. It does happen—on occasion—that through the text the Spirit teaches and guides and heals so that the text yields something other than an echo of ourselves. It does happen in prayer and study that believers are led to what is "strange and new." It does happen that preachers in sermon preparation and in utterance are led to utter beyond what they set out to do.

It does happen that churches in council, sessions, and other courts are led beyond themselves, powered beyond prejudice, liberated beyond convention, overwhelmed by the capacity for new risks.

It does happen; it happens among faithful charismatics who frighten us Calvinists but who are led to newness. It has happened in Rome, with a push toward "separated brothers and sisters," including Jews, in ways we have not. I have seen it happen in a Bible study led by an Aboriginal woman in the Australian outback who in ways primitive to me saw clearly about the gospel. And even among

Calvinists, so well defended against the Spirit, it happens in leaps over old barriers and tall buildings, in acts of generosity that defy capitalist parsimony, in reconciliation across lines of repugnance and abhorrence, in acts of forgiveness of unfathomable hate and resentment.

Such newness might have happened without the text, of course, because the wind blows where it will. But it does happen in and through the text—new resolve, new vision, new assurance, new summons. And we say, "I don't know what came over us." It is the wind in the words that comes over us, not one more grudging echo of us, but a word from out beyond, and the world begins again, "very good" indeed. We find, on such strange occasions, that not all of our historical criticism or all of our canonical reductionism, not all our moral pretense or all of our careless receptivity, not all of that or any of that can withstand the force. Because we are not speaking here of reasoned categories, but of the holy Wind that blows and destroys and makes new. The script of the book is a host and launching pad for the wind among us that the world cannot evoke and the church cannot resist.

Important

Biblical interpretation, done with imagination, willing to risk ideological distortion, open to the inspiring Spirit, is important. I would say "urgent," except that I am seeking to maintain the symmetry of the "I" terms. The importance of biblical interpretation, however, is not primarily in order to seize control of the church. It is rather that the world may have access to the good truth of the God who creates, redeems, and consummates. Of course, that missional intention is important (urgent) in every circumstance and season, and so the church at its most faithful has always understood that reading Scripture is for the sake of the missional testimony of the church to the news for the world.

But we may say more particularly and more precisely that the reading of the Bible, in all its truthfulness, is now urgent because our society is sore tempted to reduce the human project to commodity, to the making of money, to the reduction of persons to objects, to the thinning of human communications to electronic icons. The threat is technique, whether "ten ways to wealth" or "six ways to sex" or whatever. Technique, in all its military modes and derivatively in every other mode, is aimed at control, the fencing out of death, the fencing out of gift, and eventually the fencing out of humanness.

Nonetheless, we dare affirm, all of us in the church together, that this lively Word is the primal antidote to technique, the primal news that fends off trivialization. Entertain the notion of thinning to control and trivialization to evade ambiguity as the major goals of our culture. Then consider that the church in its disputatious anxiety is sorely tempted to join the choice for technique, to thin the Bible and make it one dimensional, deeply tempted to trivialization by acting as though the Bible is important because it may resolve some disruptive social inconvenience. The dispute tends to reduce what is rich and dangerous in the book to knowable technique, and what is urgent and immense to what is exhaustible trivia.

Well, it's too important for that because the dangers of the world are too great and the expectations of God are too large. What if liberals and conservatives in the church, for all their disagreement, would agree and put their energies to the main truth against the main threat? This is not to sneak in a victory about gays and lesbians for anybody, but to say that the issues before God's creation (of which we are stewards) are immense; those issues shame us in the church when our energy is deployed only to settle our anxieties. Shame, shame! Take a look at the real issues. We all know the list. What this script does is to insist that the world is not without God, not without the holy gift of life rooted in love. And yet we, in the meantime, twitter!

Conclusion

My verse goes like this:

> . . . A lamp to my feet . . .
> a light to my path.

It is a lamp and light to fend off the darkness. It is for feet and path, on the way in venture. The darkness is real, and the light is for walking boldly, faithfully in the dark we do not and cannot control.

In this crisis, the church will usefully consider what it is that is entrusted peculiarly to us with the book. If we renege on this trust, we may find that,

> instead of apostolic inherency, we settle for what is familiar;
>
> instead of interpretation, we reduce to monologue;
>
> instead of imagination, we have private fantasy;
>
> instead of facing ideology, we absolutize our anxiety;
>
> instead of inspiration, we win control;
>
> instead of importance, we end with trivialization.

There are important decisions to be made that are not partisan or sectarian, not liberal or conservative, but profoundly evangelical, and so to be made in freedom and joy.

Consider this voice from German piety outside Presbyterianism:

In essentials, unity.

It is not in doubt among us concerning the God who creates, redeems, and consummates—good news indeed!

In nonessentials, liberty.

Nonessentials, matters never settled by the apostles, or by councils.

In all things—in things essential and things nonessential—charity.

> Love is patient and kind, love is not envious or boastful, or arrogant or rude. It does not insist on its own way; it is not irritable or resentful. . . . Love bears all things, believes all things, hopes all things, endures all things. . . . And now abide faith, hope, and love, these three, and the greatest of these is love. (1 Cor. 13:4–5a, 7, 13)

In all things charity.

Recently, an Israeli journalist in Jerusalem commented on the fracturing dispute in Israel over who constitutes a real Jew—orthodox, conservative, or reformed. And said he about the dispute, "If any Jew wins, all Jews lose." Think about it: "If any Presbyterian wins, all Presbyterians lose."

In all things charity.

Notes

1. The phrase is an allusion to the famous essay of Karl Barth, "The Strange, New World within the Bible," in *The Word of God and the Word of Man* (New York: Harper & Brothers, 1957), 28–50.

2. While many folk in many traditions lay claim to this aphorism, I have it on the authority of my colleague, Lowell Zuck, that its origin is deep in German pietism.

3. My first reading out of the generativity of von Rad was in a little noticed book by B. Davie Napier, *From Faith to Faith: Essays on Old Testament Literature* (New York: Harper & Brothers, 1955). It was this book that decided for me a life of study in the Old Testament.

4. I deliberately make allusion to Martin Luther, "A Treatise on Christian Liberty," in *Three Treatises* (Philadelphia: Muhlenberg Press, 1943), 251–90.

5. The hiddenness, of course, pertains no less to the disclosure of God in Jesus of Nazareth, a truth not given to "flesh and blood" (Matt. 16:17).

6. Nor did Luther intend such self-interpretation, for all of the popular misunderstanding of his emancipation of the text from the hold of the church's magisterium.

7. See, e.g., Jon D. Levenson, *Creation and the Persistence of Evil: The Jewish Drama of Divine Omnipotence* (San Francisco: Harper & Row, 1988), 131–568.

8. See Gerhard von Rad, "Endeavors to Restore the Past," in *Old Testament Theology I* (San Francisco: Harper & Brothers, 1962), 69–77, 219–31; and Martin Noth, "The 'Re-Presentation' of the Old Testament in Proclamation," in *Essays on Old Testament Hermeneutics*, ed. Claus Westermann (Richmond: John Knox Press, 1963), 76–88. On Moses as the engine of interpretation, see Walter Brueggemann, *Theology of the Old Testament: Testimony, Dispute, Advocacy* (Minneapolis: Fortress Press, 1997), 578–90.

9. Herbert Donner, "Jesaja lvi 1–7: ein Abrogationsfall innerhalb des Kanons—Implikationen und Konsequenzen," *Supplements to Vetus Testamentum* 36 (1985): 81–95.

10. See Michael Fishbane, *Biblical Interpretation in Ancient Israel* (Oxford: Clarendon Press, 1985), 284.

11. The literature on the subject is immense and growing. See among the better representative examples, Sean McDonagh, *To Care for the Earth: A Call to a New Theology* (Quezon City, Philippines: Claretian Publications, 1986); and Carol J. Dempsey and Russell A. Butkus, eds., *All Creation Is Groaning: An Interdisciplinary Vision for Life in a Sacred Universe* (Collegeville, Minn.: Liturgical Press, 1999).

12. George Steiner, *Real Presences* (Chicago: University of Chicago Press, 1989), 225. The polyvalence of Jewish interpretation has been forcefully exposited by James L. Kugel, *The Bible as It Was* (Cambridge: Harvard University Press, 1997).

13. See my summary of the force of imagination in interpretation, *Texts under Negotiation: The Bible and Postmodern Imagination* (Minneapolis: Fortress Press, 1993).

14. On the theme, see Walter Brueggemann, "The Faithfulness of Otherwise," in *Testimony to Otherwise* (St. Louis: Chalice Press, 2001). My phrase intends to allude to the phrasing of Emmanuel Levinas.

15. On the parables as a mode of generativity for the future, see Paul Ricoeur, "Biblical Hermeneutics," *Semeia* 4 (1975): 114–45; and "The Bible and Imagination," in *Figuring the Sacred: Religion, Narrative, and Imagination,* ed. Mark I. Wallace (Minneapolis: Fortress Press, 1995), 144–66.

16. On the category of "wonder," see Martin Buber, *Moses* (Atlantic Highlands, N.J.: Humanities Press International, 1946), especially 75–76; and my discussion of Buber's insight, *Abiding Astonishment: Psalms, Modernity, and the Making of History,* Literary Currents in Biblical Interpretation (Louisville, Ky.: Westminster John Knox Press, 1991), 30–33 and passim.

17. Karl Barth, *Church Dogmatics,* III/1, *The Doctrine of Creation* (Edinburgh: T. & T. Clark, 1958), 81, 91. See the discussion of the cruciality of imagination after Wittgenstein, and especially on Barth, by Fergus Kerr, *Theology after Wittgenstein* (London: SPCK, 1997).

18. For an example of "ideology critique," see David Penchansky, *The Betrayal of God: Ideological Conflict in Job,* Literary Currents in Biblical Interpretation (Louisville, Ky.: Westminster John Knox Press, 1990).

19. Distinctions can be made in the use of "ideology" in a Marxian sense (as here) and after the manner of Clifford Geertz. A helpful guide on the concept is Paul Ricoeur, *Lectures on Ideology and Utopia* (New York: Columbia University Press, 1986).

20. The passionate intentionality of the authors of texts has been forced upon the awareness of biblical scholarship by Norman K. Gottwald, *The Tribes of Yahweh: A Sociology of the Religion of Liberated Israel, 1250–1050 B.C.* (Maryknoll, N.Y.: Orbis Books, 1979). After Gottwald, a host of scholars have joined issue on the matter.

21. On what follows, see Walter Brueggemann, *Texts under Negotiation*, 61–64.
22. On "felt threats" as propulsions for interpretation, see Walter Brueggemann, "Contemporary Old Testament Theology: A Contextual Prospectus," *Dialog* 38 (spring 1999): 108–16.
23. See Carolyn Pressler, *The View of Women Found in the Deuteronomic Family Laws*, BZAW 216 (Berlin: Walter De Gruyter, 1993).
24. See Henri Mottu, "Jeremiah vs. Hananiah: Ideology and Truth in Old Testament Prophecy," in *The Bible and Liberation: Political and Social Hermeneutics*, ed. Norman K. Gottwald (Maryknoll, N.Y.: Orbis Books, 1983), 235–51.

Struggling with Scripture

William C. Placher

Professor of Philosophy and Religion
Wabash College

I received my first Bible when I was a kid, back in Peoria, for graduating from the fourth-grade Sunday school class. It has been with me ever since. From reading the Bible, more than anywhere else, I have come to know Jesus, my Lord and Savior. If I did not know Jesus, I cannot imagine how my life would make much sense, or how I would have had the hope to sustain me in times of darkness. So you need to know that I do not speak about the Bible as a neutral, objective scholar, but as someone who finds himself on bad days clinging like a drowning person to this book.

Some people would therefore think that, in addressing the Covenant Network of Presbyterians, I have come to the wrong place. If I really wanted to talk to Bible-believing Christians, they would argue, then I should have gone somewhere else—to the Southern Baptists, maybe, or at least the more conservative Presbyterians. In *The Word: Imagining the Gospel in Modern America*, Ann Monroe writes, "For conservatives, the Bible is in charge. . . . For [liberals], the Bible is whatever the reader makes of it: not a source of truth, but a taking-off place in the search for truth beyond it."[1] Frame the issue that way, and I find myself wanting to be a conservative.

Yet her view is common enough. Rank people along a line with "fundamentalists" at one end, as the people who take the Bible really, really seriously, and then down the continuum to those who take it really seriously, those who take it seriously, those who take it less seriously, and those who scarcely attend to it at all. Such a scheme characteristically tries to put most of us in this room somewhere near the end of the line.

My problem is that none of the places on that continuum, as usually defined, feels like home to me. I am hoping and expecting that many of you find that such a scheme of classification does not quite do you justice either. I certainly would not describe myself as a fundamentalist, yet I do not think that I am somehow less committed to the Bible on that account. I would not want to put too much weight on my own example, for I am very conscious of my own failures to live a life that consistently follows the teachings of Scripture. But even some of those who seem to me most committed to living out the biblical message in their lives, given this way of classifying, would count as "not taking the Bible very seriously."

How can that be? I guess my explanation would be the thesis I want to present to you today, namely, that taking the Bible most seriously means one does not affirm its truth apart from struggling to understand its meaning.

The Genres of the Bible

To explain, let's start with an easy example. Jesus tells how a certain man went down from Jerusalem to Jericho and was set upon by thieves. A priest and a Levite walked on by, but a Samaritan stopped to help him. We do not check the records of the Jerusalem-Jericho highway patrol to see whether this really happened. Even if we had those records, we would not feel the need to examine them. We recognize that Jesus is here not reporting historical fact but telling a story that will make a point, a parable. In understanding the story *as* a parable, we understand what it really means.

Similarly, a little reflection suggests that when the book of Jonah tells how all the people of Ninevah heard the word of the Lord and repented, any Israelite would have recognized that something funny was going on. The Assyrians, who had their capital at Ninevah, were among Israel's great enemies. Even usually nonjudgmental historians admit that they were a militaristic, rather nasty lot. There is no record of any dramatic change of values in their society, and any Jew would have known that the Assyrians remained as unrepentently aggressive as ever.

Thus, when the author of Jonah tells the story of this prophet who brought all the people of the Assyrian capital to repent, it would have hit Jews like a vegetarian today saying, "Let me tell you the story of the guy who talked McDonald's out of selling hamburgers." They would have recognized at once that this story was something other than history.

That recognition need not imply that the story is "untrue." We learn more truth about humanity from *War and Peace* than from *People* magazine's latest news about the lives of celebrities. But it is truth conveyed in a different way, in something more like an extended parable than a historian's careful account. Therefore, if someone insists on the historical truth of Jonah—conversion of Ninevah, big fish, and all—they are not taking the Bible more seriously than the rest of us. They are misunderstanding it.

I am, of course, sliding past a great many difficult hermeneutical questions about the relation of the meaning of a text to the intention of its author, or the role and character of its implied audience, or how a particular book in the Bible may have a different meaning in its context as part of the canon. For now, I simply want to make the relatively simple point that the Bible comes to us in a variety of genres:

> Paul lists people to whom Jesus appeared, including one group of five hundred, and he says that some of them are still alive. In this case, we are reading the words of a man who wants to persuade his readers about something that recently really happened, and he is citing his witnesses.

> In the opening chapters of Genesis, on the other hand, as Karl Barth observed, people live for hundreds of years. Animals talk. We are in a world not clearly connected with historical events. The text gives us a lot of signals that this is something more like fable than modern history, what Barth and Martin Buber before him called "saga," a poetic rendering of primeval truths about humanity.

> Jesus speaks in parables. The book of Jonah offers us something like an extended parable. And so on.

These are all kinds of different genres. The genre of a particular text shapes its meaning. Its meaning determines what it is for it to be true. And therefore I cannot properly affirm its truth without thinking about its genre. If I am to believe in the story of the good Samaritan in the right way, I need to understand that it is a parable and not a crime report.

Data, the robot in one of the *Star Trek* series, cannot understand jokes. He takes them literally (or at least he did; I think he was catching on, but I stopped following the series). He is or was not a good audience for a comedian, and he would frustrate a comedian if he said, "But I took you more seriously and literally than anyone else did." His literalism does not mean that he is the most faithful audience for a joke; it means he misunderstands.

Sometimes, to be sure, the genre of a biblical text, and the rules that apply to that genre, may remain mysterious to us. The clues within a given culture as to what sort of story we are about to hear can be subtle. For instance, if I had begun my remarks today by saying, "A minister, a priest, and a rabbi went out in a boat," all of you would have been expecting a joke. If I had begun, "Once upon a time," you would have anticipated a fairy tale or, failing that, an ironic takeoff on a fairy tale.

Think for a minute about what complicated narrative analyses you would have been performing. Imagine trying to explain to someone from a completely different culture why you knew a joke was coming as soon as I said, "A minister, a priest, and a rabbi." Cultural sensitivities—some justified, some exaggerated—make us nervous about ethnic humor, so the generation of our grandchildren may not anticipate a joke if they hear those same words. Yet you could read an unabridged dictionary, the *Encyclopaedia Britannica*, Fowler's *Modern English Usage*, and any number of other reference books without finding the information that "A minister, a priest, and a rabbi . . ." means "joke coming."

Think then how many signals about genre and meaning in the Bible probably go completely over our heads. We no longer know the cultural clues. Sometimes scholars can help explain them to us. But sometimes even the best scholars are missing things or have to confess their puzzlement. Listen, for instance, to a few verses from chapter 1 of Revelation:

> I was in the spirit on the Lord's day, and I heard
> behind me a loud voice like a trumpet saying, "Write
> in a book what you see. . . ." Then I turned to see
> whose voice it was that spoke to me, and on turning
> I saw seven golden lampstands, and in the midst of
> the lampstands I saw one like the Son of Man. (Rev.
> 1:10–11a, 12–13a)

Now I am sure there are biblical scholars smarter and
more learned than I am—Walter Brueggemann and Brian
Blount, just for a start—but how can any of us recover
with confidence what that passage would have meant to an
early-second-century Christian community?

Would they, for instance, have thought this was a report
of an actual vision, or more a literary construction, or
what? We cannot be sure. There are times when, the
Westminster Confession reminds us, we need to turn
from less clear passages to clearer ones in our interpretation of the Bible. One of the convictions guiding the
Reformed tradition in these matters has always been that
those things needful for salvation will be clear enough if
we are studying Scripture as a whole. If we study the whole
Bible, its central concerns come through clearly enough.
We learn that we are all sinners, that God loves us anyway,
and that knowing our salvation rests on grace frees us to
live in the service of God and neighbor without worrying
about how we will be rewarded.

What the Bible Teaches

If we are trying to interpret a particular passage, however,
we have to start by asking about its meaning. So far, my
examples of the meaning of texts have mostly concerned
narrative passages, and a generation or two ago that was

where arguments about biblical authority primarily focused. Did this miracle really happen? Was this story true? Those were the issues most debated by, for instance, Bultmann and his critics. Increasingly, however, our most passionate debates about biblical authority focus on the moral injunctions in Scripture. Is this really a sin? Is this claim about how we ought to live our lives really true?

No American theologian, I believe, has thought about these issues more carefully than—I am about to surprise some of you—that stalwart of old Princeton orthodoxy, Charles Hodge. I do not always agree with him, but he was a great thinker, and he still repays rereading.

Even in asserting doctrines of biblical infallibility and plenary inspiration, Hodge introduced qualifications. The sacred writers, he said, "were infallible" only "for the special purpose for which they were employed." "As to all matters of science, philosophy, and history, they stood on the same level as their contemporaries." So Hodge accepted that Isaiah made false assumptions about astronomy and Paul forgot how many people he had actually converted at Corinth. But these were not the matters they were *teaching*. "We must distinguish between what the sacred writers themselves thought or believed, and what they teach. They may have believed [for example] that the sun moves round the earth, but they do not so teach."[2]

Hodge wanted to make sure that theologians did not make fools of themselves by trying to defend the indefensible. He remembered earlier battles in which Christians had insisted that the sun goes around the earth, because the Bible seems to say so. No, Hodge insisted—some of the authors of the Bible may have *assumed* that the earth is at the center of the planetary system, but that was not the point they were trying to make, and not what they were *teaching*.

Hodge, for that matter, had no problem with the idea, coming to the fore in the evolutionary science of his day, that the earth had existed for millions of years. The authors of Genesis may have believed in a much shorter time-span of world history, he admitted, but they did not teach it. Therefore, we need not believe it in order to believe in the truth of the Bible.

Hodge's distinction has intriguing analogies to Rudolf Bultmann's later line between the kerygmatic kernel of the gospel and the mythological husk which we can appropriately cast off from it. Many of us think that Bultmann cast off too much—that, for instance, it won't do to say that Jesus rose in the faith of the earliest disciples and to dismiss the empty tomb stories as not part of the kerygma. And many of us think that Hodge didn't go far enough, that he accepted too much from the Bible as teaching that we have to believe. What is worth noting, however, is that across a wide theological spectrum *everyone* agrees that you have to draw a line somewhere between the cultural assumptions in which the message of the Bible is presented and the message that is presented in them. We argue about where to draw the line, and those arguments are important, but all parties in such arguments agree that a line needs to be drawn.

Still, it's a tricky distinction, isn't it? Consider the application of Hodge's method to a different case, one of great concern to our denomination in his time. In the days of slavery, some Presbyterians as well as non-Presbyterians cited Paul's Letter to Philemon as teaching that owning slaves is morally acceptable. After all, Paul does not demand that Philemon free his slave Onesimus.

We might say, in response, that Paul was assuming the social reality of slavery in his time, but what he *teaches* in the letter has at its core his appeal that in Christ a master might be called to be a brother even to his slave. The let-ter teaches about a transformation of the nature of human relations, not about the acceptability of slavery. Along the way, we might also emphasize the differences between slavery in the ancient world and in the American South and ask whether what Paul discussed was really the same thing as slavery as it existed in America in 1850.

These distinctions cannot be drawn easily, however, and the danger is always that we will bend over backward either to rescue Paul or to preserve our own prejudices. It would certainly be embarrassing if Paul supported slavery, so are we trying to weasel him out of it? In other cases, are we seeking to avoid his challenge to our cultural assump-tions? Perhaps. Yet if drawing such distinctions between what is taught and what is merely assumed is difficult, that does not make it impossible. I think we can, sometimes at least, with appropriate caution and self-criticism, draw lines between the point of the text (what it teaches) and the assumptions the author brought from his time and place to express that point. I would not claim Hodge's way of putting it as the last or best word in these matters, but I think it is not a bad starting point.

So let's take a harder case, and one we are all thinking about these days. In chapter 1 of Romans, Paul is discussing the righteousness of God. Is such righteousness compatible, he asks, with the fact that some people have never heard the good news of God's revelation in the law and the prophets or in Christ? Yes, it is, he answers. "Ever since the creation of the world his eternal power and divine nature, invisible though they are, have been understood and seen through the things he has made. So they are without excuse; for though they knew God, they did not honor him as God or give thanks to him, but they became futile in their thinking, and their senseless minds were darkened" (Rom. 1:20–21).

In other words, the reality of creation, visible to all, should have been enough to indicate to people the existence of some sort of God worthy of worship, and it was because of their sin that they could not see that truth. Therefore, the failure to know God is their fault.

Because of that failure, in turn, two things went wrong. First, they fell into worshiping idols, "and they exchanged the glory of the immortal God for images resembling a mortal human being or birds or four-footed animals or reptiles" (Rom. 1:23). They replaced the mystery of God with images that they could describe and get hold of. Second, "because they exchanged the truth about God for a lie and worshiped and served the creature rather than the Creator," "therefore God gave them up in the lusts of their hearts to impurity" (vv. 25, 24). Specifically, "Their women exchanged natural intercourse for unnatural, and in the same way also the men, giving up natural intercourse with women, were consumed with passion for one another" (vv. 26b–27a). Furthermore, "They were filled with every kind of wickedness, evil, covetousness, malice. Full of envy, murder, strife, deceit, craftiness, they are gossips, slanderers, God-haters, insolent, haughty, boastful, inventors of evil, rebellious toward parents, foolish, faithless, heartless, ruthless" (vv. 29–31).

I have quoted Paul at such length because part of my argument is that we understand texts only in context. Remembering the whole arc of Paul's argument allows us to raise a question: Is Paul teaching that same-sex intercourse is wrong? Or is he *teaching* something about the relation between human responsibility, the failure to worship the true God, and ethical faults, and in the process *assuming*, as a Jew moving out into Hellenistic culture in the first century would have, that same-sex intercourse is a good example of sin? Is this last point an example of something taught, or is it an example of a shared assumption of a particular culture, taken for granted in the process of making a point about something else?

I think that's a good question. I happen to believe that it was merely assumption, not teaching—that Paul's reference to homosexuality isn't what he here teaches but an example he draws from the cultural assumptions of his time to illustrate his thesis about the relation of God, sin, and human responsibility. I note in passing that the two best commentaries on Romans I know—those of Martin Luther and Karl Barth—discuss this passage without directly mentioning sex at all. Though their authors certainly thought homosexuality sinful, they seem to assume that the *teaching* here addresses other topics. Still, I am very conscious that I bring a set of prejudices, hopes, and concerns to the matter, just as anyone else does. I have good reasons to mistrust my own conclusions.

My primary intent here, therefore (given limited space and my own limits in expertise), is not to answer the question about the meaning of this text but to say that it is good to ask what it means before we demand that people believe it in order to be faithful to Scripture. Indeed, asking about the *meaning* of such difficult passages is the kind of question we ought, as Christians and as Presbyterians, to be considering together. Such questions do not, notice, concern how seriously we take the authority of the Bible. People who take its authority equally seriously can disagree about its meaning.

There are those who would deny any value to debates about the meaning of such a passage. On one side, some would say that we need not struggle with such complex issues because Romans 1:26 says that same-sex intercourse is an example of impurity, and that settles the matter. But I have tried to remind you that we ask complex questions about the meaning and context of individual verses all the time when we are interpreting the Bible. We have to, in order to understand it. There is no reason to stop our normal practice when we reach this particular passage.

On the other side, some would say that Paul was wrong, we know he was wrong, he was the product of a patriarchal culture, we can disregard him, and who cares what he was teaching and what he was just assuming? To them, I have to say—I care. As I have said already, it is through knowing the Christ of whom I learn in the Bible that I make sense of my life and have my hope. So I need to be able to trust what the Bible teaches. Moreover, it is with the Bible that I try from time to time to challenge myself and my fellow Christians to rethink our comfortable lives in the light of what following Christ might call us to do. I do not know how to demand that others take the Bible seriously when it challenges their beliefs if I feel I can dismiss the passages that discomfort me.

I therefore do think that we have to struggle with questions like: What is the point of this passage? What is it calling us to do? Where is it going? And in contrast, where is it just assuming something that people of that time and culture would have assumed, in passing, as it heads toward its real goal?

For that matter, just as we needed to ask whether "slavery" referred to the same institution in the ancient world and the antebellum American South, so we need to ask what people were doing that Paul found objectionable. Same-sex intercourse in the Hellenistic world seems often to have been something done by people who were in other parts of their lives heterosexual. It often involved boys young enough that we would call them children, and accounts of it regularly emphasize how it asserted the power of one partner over another rather than an equality in love. Paul saw all this and opposed it, but can we be sure just what part of it he opposed, and how he might have reacted to very different forms of homosexuality in our society?

I do not claim that such distinctions are easy to make or that such questions are easy to answer. Hodge's examples of the way the biblical authors assumed the erroneous beliefs of their culture concerned physical science. We have learned things about the solar system, he concluded, that the writers of the Bible did not know, and he made the argument that those writers merely assumed the mistaken science of their time. They did not teach it. I would propose that we might also say that we can learn new things from the social sciences—about human psychology, for instance—and then go back and see that Paul or other biblical authors were sometimes simply assuming the social science of *their* time on their way to making a point about something else. Some folks will doubt that social science really gives us new truths in the way that physical science does. Others will argue that the line between truths of social science and faith cannot be drawn the way the line between natural science and faith can. Those are issues worth arguing. But, again, they are not arguments that divide serious Bible believers from those who take Scripture less seriously.

Being Consistent

It seems to me that our denomination and recent public discussion of biblical interpretation in general have too often not been very good at looking at these kinds of argument. Indeed, with respect to our denomination, here I fear I have to be a little harsh, though with deep regret.

Let me be a bit facetious first. You may recall that Paul's list of the sins into which humanity has fallen includes not only same-sex intercourse but also gossiping. According to the *Book of Order*, people engaging unrepentantly in same-sex intercourse cannot be ordained Presbyterian elders. But what about unrepentant gossips? I don't know about your congregation, but in mine back in Indiana, I am not sure we could get a session together if we enforced a limitation there. Just to make clear that I am not making fun of other people, let me admit that I would not be able to serve on the session.

I am not entirely serious in raising this issue, of course, but I do have a serious point to make: Even if we conclude that all the activities on Paul's list are sins, there remains the question of whether some are more serious than others. Those who judge same-sex intercourse as obviously the most serious of all are not deriving that conclusion simply from what Paul says.

Indeed, I do not think one could read through the Bible honestly and judge homosexuality to be a very important issue in its pages. So why has it come to be such an important issue in the life of our church? Some would answer that people are claiming the right to engage in same-sex intercourse without having that count as sin at all. Yet are there not many in our culture who pursue greed and injustice unapologetically? The Bible condemns such sins much more often. Why is our focus not on them?

Consider another specific case. Jesus' assertion in Matthew 5:32 that "anyone who divorces his wife, except on the ground of unchastity, causes her to commit adultery; and whoever marries a divorced woman commits adultery" seems to me at least as clear and straightforward as any biblical assertion concerning same-sex intercourse. Yet it does not, as far as I can see, have much effect in the life of our denomination today.

It might be said that one can repent of divorce and

remarry but continued same-sex intercourse is obviously unrepentant. But let's not trivialize repentance. If we never even raise the question whether divorced people might remain celibate for the sake of their children, for instance, are we talking seriously about repentance? Such an expectation would seem analogous to the demand that gay people lead celibate lives, yet many who would not dream of insisting on the one firmly demand the other.

I think one can work out a way of interpreting Matthew 5:32 that would accept remarriage after divorce as sometimes the least evil of available options. I do not believe, however, that we as a denomination have worked out any clear distinction between this case and same-sex intercourse on theological or scriptural grounds. I think we make the distinction because too many powerful and respectable people in our church and society are divorced, whereas in many parts of our society it is still socially acceptable to treat homosexuals with contempt. In other words, the lines we draw flow out of the cultural values and power relations of our society, not from any interpretive strategy we consistently apply to biblical texts.

For that matter, when our Southern Baptist brothers and sisters reaffirm the Letter to Titus's assertion that wives should be submissive to their husbands, we Presbyterians mostly either laugh or burst out in fury. I certainly do not propose that we should follow them down that road. But why is it that we take Romans 1 more seriously than Titus 2? For that matter, what about Jesus' judgment that it is easier for a camel to pass through the eye of a needle than for a rich man to get into the kingdom of heaven? Here again, I concede there are ways of understanding the texts in wider contexts and so on. My puzzle is why we seem to do that with some texts and not with others. And my sad conclusion is that if a given group is powerful enough, then we ignore the passages that criticize them. Homosexuals, however, remain a marginalized group in our society and our church, so we go ahead and take literally the passages that seem to condemn them.

Once it gets put that way, it does seem kind of awful, doesn't it? I think it would be more intellectually consistent and morally responsible to be either more conservative or more liberal than we currently are. As Søren Kierkegaard said of his feelings about the church of his time, I am not for severity or for laxity, but simply for honesty.

If anything, after all, an interpretive favoritism for the powerful seems the opposite of Jesus' own practice. He so often forcefully condemned forms of sin that were treated as more or less respectable behavior in his time and place while viewing rather casually the sins that generated the most contempt in his society. He denounced the hypocrisy of the Pharisees far more than the sins of prostitutes or tax collectors. He was, in other words, apt to be more forgiving of the relatively powerless or the outcast.

Still, I would not want, as some theologians of liberation have done, to try to develop that into a general principle. I do not think it works to say, "Always take more seriously the passages that condemn powerful people." For one thing, you have to decide who is powerful and who is oppressed. My friend Miroslav Volf, out of his experience growing up in the former Yugoslavia, has pointed out that, once you start down that road, there are often many parties that can claim to be oppressed. Remember what you did to us last week. Remember what you did to us last year. And then there's what you did to us in the sixteenth century. And so it goes.

For that matter, in Jesus' context, should we consider tax collectors as the objects of general scorn or as part of the power structure? They were probably both. People do not always divide neatly into oppressed and oppressors, and Jesus resisted making such divisions clear-cut. But we can say, I think, that interpretations that consistently favor the powerful rather clearly do not follow Jesus' practice. If we seek to be followers of Jesus and mean to give any-one the benefit of the doubt, it should be those our soci-ety is inclined to condemn. Similarly, practices that drive away rather than welcome, that set strict limits to the grace of God rather than marvel at its superabundance—such practices are not in accord with the practices of Jesus.

What then is the alternative to letting the values and power structures of our society so shape the way we read the Bible? I can only propose the classic Reformed prac-tice of interpreting the Bible in the light of the Bible. Of course, we always bring our questions and our assumptions to the text, but that need not mean that we inevitably close ourselves off from having the text surprise us. The power of masterful biblical interpreters like Walter Brueggemann or Brian Blount, Phyllis Trible or James Cone—or John Calvin—is that they bring us to read the Bible in a way that we had not expected and yet, after we have traveled with them, we go back to the text and see what they have pointed to there, clear as day. When we cannot find such insight, we can turn to the old rule of interpreting the less clear in the light of the more clear.

We need to struggle with challenging texts in their immediate context and then eventually in the context of the whole of Scripture, connect them in the richest web we can imagine of all that the Bible offers us, in the way that clas-sical interpreters like Augustine or Calvin did so powerfully. In that context, then, we start to decide what constitutes teaching and what constitutes the cultural assumptions in which the given teaching happened to be cast. This is diffi-cult, and no method for doing it is infallible. With respect to one passage, we can be guided by our sense of themes within the Bible as a whole, but, even at that, sometimes we will, if we are honest, simply remain puzzled.

With respect to same-sex intercourse, I myself think it falls into the category of what Paul and others assumed from their culture, not what the Bible teaches. Making that case, as I noted earlier, would be a topic for another time, and it is a case others have already made with more scholarly expertise than I could bring to bear. What I want to insist here is simply that our conclusion on this issue ought to be reached by methods we consistently apply to other texts, too, and that at the moment our denomination does not seem to me to be doing that.

As Christians, we struggle with biblical texts, and our very commitment to the struggle is the sign of our faithfulness to this book. Christians can learn from Jews, I think, how the commitment to wrestle, even angrily, with the texts manifests faithfulness. Even as we keep brooding over particular passages, though, we find that this book, which sometimes so frustrates us or angers us or mystifies us, is shaping the way we see the world and live our lives and ever again is reintroducing us to the God in whom we believe. In a lifetime of reading the Bible, in trying to understand it, we find that we are enabled to live more fully as Christians.

That is what it means to take the Bible seriously: to struggle over a lifetime of reading or preaching, to try to see the relation of parts to whole, to admit what we cannot understand, to recognize all the different ways the genres of the Bible can mean and teach. If you are doing that, do not let anyone tell you that, when they take one passage out of context and insist on its literal meaning, they are being more faithful to the Bible than you are.

On the other hand, if you are not living with your Bible, reading it every day, worrying out the passages that anger or mystify you, preaching (if you are a preacher) on texts that make you deeply uncomfortable, making it clear that your preaching starts with the text and not with what you wanted to say anyway—if you are not doing these things, then maybe you ought to start.

Part of the function of this gathering is to give the occasion for public and private discussions of political strategy concerning the future of our denomination, and I recognize the need for such strategizing even as I defer to those more expert in it than I. But if that is all we do, even if we do it with great success, we will not have abandoned the principle that power shapes our interpretations. We will change only the current reality of who has the most power.

So might we, in addition to our political strategizing, commit ourselves to this: that in our preaching and teaching, our lives and our conversations, we mean to be manifestly Bible-believing Christians, yielding priority to no one in our fidelity to this book. We will be so engaged with Scripture that no one else can credibly claim that they are the Presbyterians who take the Bible seriously. We insist, indeed, that in believing what the Bible means and teaches, rather than in misunderstandings of it, we are *most* faithful to it. We vow to manifest ourselves as the people who take the Bible most seriously, who struggle hardest to be faithful to it, recognizing that faithfulness always does involve struggle and the recognition of complexity, even as we find this book shaping our lives and our faith and guiding us to the knowledge and love of God.

Notes

1. Ann Monroe, *The Word: Imagining the Gospel in Modern America* (Louisville, Ky.: Westminster John Knox Press, 2000), 212.
2. Charles Hodge, *Systematic Theology*, 3 vols. (1872; reprint, Grand Rapids, Mich.: Wm. B. Eerdmans, 1992), 1:165, 170.

The Last Word
on Biblical Authority

Brian K. Blount

Associate Professor of New Testament
Princeton Theological Seminary

W hen a friend asked what the title of my lecture would be, I said tentatively, testing the waters a bit but still eager to get his reaction, "The Last Word on Biblical Authority." He chuckled and said, "I hope they get the joke." "What joke?" I thought. I wondered for a moment whether I was so clever that I had ended up talking over my own head and thought, "There's no joke; it's a conference that will address issues of biblical authority and I'm up last."

But there is a joke. We all know people who for some unknown reason just have to have the last word on any and every subject. We can't leave unless we hear their voices ringing in our ears. No matter what has happened in the intervening argument, they haven't heard, they haven't cared, because they know they're right, and all they want to do is let us get what we have to say out of our system so they can get in their word, *the last word*. As far as they are concerned, their word is the authoritative word on which we ought to build our lives.

Many people treat the biblical words that way, believing that those words, all of them, must always be the last words standing. Now in matters of faith—in matters of understanding our human relationship before God and God's moves to nurture, develop, restructure, and refine that relationship through the prophetic and incarnate Word—most of Christendom, I think, agrees that those inspired words are lasting words. But in matters of the proper way to appropriate those words of faith *ethically*, there is and has always been considerable discussion and debate.

This is because deep down we know that even the inspired biblical authors, when they applied God's prophetic and incarnate Word to their very human situations, allowed those situations to influence how they heard God and therefore how they talked to each other. In the biblical world of the first century, for example, generally speaking, slavery was a given, women were understood to be inferior to men, and the power of the empire demanded allegiance or at least acquiescence from those who wanted to survive. The many authoritative New Testament biblical words that sanctioned slavery (Eph. 6:5; Col. 3:22; Titus 2:9; 1 Pet. 2:18), devalued women (1 Cor. 11; 14:34–35), or encouraged an almost blind obedience to the state (Rom. 13; 1 Pet. 2:13–15) are testimony to the fact that the biblical authors were themselves creatures of their contexts who, just as we do today, felt the inspiration of God and then translated the Word of God for their lives *through* those contexts.

What are we to say about the biblical words being the last word in such cases? There have been many esteemed men and women of faith who argued that those words on slavery ought to be the last word and who thereby defended slavery and the enslavement of black people in the United States up to, through, and even beyond the horror of the Civil War. There are many esteemed men and women of faith who have argued and continue to argue that the words on the secondary status of women are the last word on the issue of ordination of women to the Christian clergy. There were many esteemed men and women of faith in the United States who, during the days of the Civil Rights movement, chastised the freedom riders and prophetic protesters because they disobeyed the governing laws of the land and who denigrated them because, instead of waiting for change to evolve slowly over time, they acted to press for an immediate allocation of equal rights.

But were those esteemed men and women of faith right?

Of course not! Because ethical biblical authority is *contextual* biblical authority. Now, what does that mean? Think of it this way: Loving God is in some ways like watching silent movies. There are kaleidoscopes of colorful emotion, juggernauts of reeling action, and narrative schemes of implied ethical direction. But there is no sound.

Yet, there *is* a voice. Every story, every power has its own voice, a way of viewing the world and being viewed by it that signals a message as much by *how* it "speaks" as by *what* it "says." Voice, though, does not necessarily require sound. It needs only an audience and a channel to reach it. The physical ear need not be involved.

That's because the human spirit is a kind of inner ear. It is the instrument upon which the reverberations of God's voice make their impact. It is the human spirit that translates what our eyes see, our fingers touch, our noses smell, our bodies experience, and our ears do *not* hear into the voice of God. That is why even though God does not talk in a way we are accustomed to hearing others talk, we are able to listen to God.

The role of the spirit is a constant. Laced into the fabric of human beings is that part of us that reaches beyond the boundaries of our flesh and blood and touches the essential voice of God's own Holy Spirit. Did you ever hear someone say a room is wired for sound? We're wired for God, wired by God with a human spirit that despite its limitations can be touched by God's Holy Spirit. In every time, in every place, in every moment of history, the spirit plays this interlocutory role. It is how we "hear" God and through this hearing, when we are fortunate, hear each other. The spirit is a constant.

The "human" is not. Being human signals contingency, limitation, and context. Because they are human, our spirits always encounter God *through the context* in which God finds us and we find ourselves. This means that each one of us as individuals or in community *always* perceives God—and what it is that God wants from us—*differently*.

God's voice, then, is like an inaudible whisper—sometimes gentle, sometimes fierce—that jangles the nerves of the human spirit until, tensed and alert, it attends to what it is that God wants to "say." That saying will be different according to the variable conditions in which the human spirits who encounter it find themselves. When that spiritual whisper grips the human spirits where they live, it becomes an incarnate Word taking up the cause of the people who encounter it *in the situations of that encounter*. It is in *this* way that God's eternal voice for all becomes a living Word exclusively *for them*. God's whisper takes on flesh.

That flesh is the human word of the human disciples who have written our biblical texts. Like all flesh, it is limited, and often the ethical words they have written are also limited to their times and their places. This means that the words of those texts ought to be challenged when we find that they were influenced by their contexts in such a way that they are damaging, and not life affirming, in a contemporary circumstance.

We're asking the question, How do we go about understanding which biblical words *live* today, and which don't? I know it's always intimidating for seminary students when such a notion comes up in a class lecture or discussion. People need some absolute, something hard and lasting, a last word on all things for all ethical situations for every ethical context imaginable. We are like Paul's babes in the faith; we need the suckling security of a milk bottle filled with authoritative assurances about what we should do and how we should live in any and every time for any and every circumstance. We don't want complexities because we're not spiritually grown up enough to handle them. We want it simple: simplified faith, simplified ethics in light of that faith. We want "do this" or "do that," "don't do this" or "don't do that." We're too often not ready for the meat of mature considerations about the words of texts that were often right for their own time twenty centuries ago but may well be wrong for our time.

We're too often the not-yet-ready-for-prime-time pietists who equate faith with God to faith in the written words of human texts. Carlos Mesters makes the case provocatively when he talks about poor Latin American peasants whose oppressed circumstances often motivate them to challenge the ethical exhortations of the biblical texts whenever those exhortations would perpetuate their oppression. So, Mesters writes, these "common people are putting the Bible in its proper place, the place where God intended it to be. They are putting it in second place. Life takes first place!"[1]

That means, then, that as far as biblical ethics are concerned, for the peasants Mesters was talking about, there is no last word on biblical authority. Why? Because the authoritative words are linked to the contexts in which they were uttered. And since we're always changing, and our contexts are always changing, the words that interpret the whisper of God's Spirit in our time must necessarily be changing as well. God, you remember Jesus saying, is a God of the living, not the dead. But a last word is necessarily a dead word. It stops listening. It stops learning. It stops living! It just wants to be repeated over and over without being informed by anything about anything that has happened between the time of its first utterance and its purported final utterance now.

We've often made the biblical words the last word in the sense that none of them can ever change. Even if the words were on the mark for a first-century community but are no longer on target for ours, even when they have become like rickety, arthritic knees that don't bend and twist so well in the new race we're running for God, we treat them as if they just started competing yesterday. A last word can't breathe; it can't endure this marathon of living with the people of God who run in the presence of God's ever-living, ever-sustaining Holy Spirit.

Making the biblical words the last word turns them into literary artifacts. Over time, any church working with such a word becomes fossilized into the past itself; it becomes an archaeological dig rather than a living faith community that celebrates seeing God say and do new things in new times.

A last word tries to mask its own insecurity about its timelessness by forcing the present to live in the past. We often hear the criticism that the church ought not to adapt to the surrounding culture but speak to it. That's a powerfully correct assertion in my mind. But the church and its believers also ought not adapt to any past culture but, rather, speak *to* it! Speak from it, yes, but also speak to it in a way that values human living *now*, before God, just as human living before God was valued in the first century. And that valuing process may well mean that words that may have been valuable in the first century must no longer be equally valued today.

Let me say it this way: *Nothing that is living is ever last.* A living word is always a beginning word. In a reality of living that believes in the word of resurrection, even the word of someone's death is a word of beginning. Even death is not the last word. That's because God is a God of the living.

A Living Word: The African American Slaves

Many people will respond to this by saying, "It hardly sounds Christian." But it is, and I'll give you two Christian examples of this kind of biblical interpretation.

The African American slaves in the United States were a community that was as faithful to the powerful message of Jesus Christ in their lives as any community in history. In spite of what they endured, what they lost, how often they were brutalized or killed, their songs, their sermons, their narratives and stories are a testimony to their faith in God's powerful presence in their lives. And even though the laws of the land—the same laws many biblical words suggested they should blindly obey—made it illegal for them to learn to read, somehow they learned the biblical stories and internalized them. God's story became their story. But they realized that human beings interpreted that story and put God's holy Word into their own con-textually influenced human words. So when slave owners talked about the Bible saying that slaves ought to obey their masters, the slaves resisted not just the slave owners but the biblical words and the biblical authors themselves. The grandmother of African American spiritualist Howard Thurman, once the dean of the chapel at Howard University, is a grand case in point. Thurman records what she once said to him:

> My regular chore was to do all of the reading for my grandmother—she could neither read nor write. . . . With a feeling of great temerity I asked her one day why it was that she would not let me read any of the Pauline letters. What she told me I shall never forget. "During the days of slavery," she said, "the master's minister would occasionally hold services for the slaves. . . . Always the white minister used as his text something from Paul. At least three or four times a year he used as a text: 'Slaves be obedient to them that are your masters . . . , as unto Christ.' Then he would go on to show how, if we were good and happy slaves, God would bless us. I promised my Maker that if I ever learned to read and if freedom ever came, I would not read that part of the Bible."[2]

Here is an illiterate woman who knows instinctively that a last word is too dead a word to keep living for her.

And then there was the group of slaves in Georgia, in 1833, who listened to a white preacher go on about Paul's text on Philemon:

> In Liberty County a group of slaves were listening to a white minister hold forth on a staple topic—the escaped slave Onesimus, and his return to his master. According to the report from Georgia, half of the Negro group walked out when the point of the ser-

mon became clear, and the other half stayed mostly
for the purpose of telling [the preacher] that they
were sure there was no such passage in the Bible.[3]

Of course, it *is* in the Bible. It's in your Bible and my Bible,
and it was in the slaves' Bible. But they contested it! They
walked out on it! Why? Because theirs was the *living* Bible.
Professor Jacquelyn Grant is correct in her assessment of
what is going on here when she writes, "What we see here
is perhaps more than a mere rejection of a White preacher's
interpretation of the Bible, but an exercise in internal critique of the Bible."[4] In other words, if the biblical words on
slavery were the last word on slavery, they were too dead a
word to keep living for them.

This doesn't mean that the New Testament text lost its
sense of authority for the slaves. But it *does* mean that their
perception of God in their midst was *more* authoritative.
The text must be in line with God's being and God's
agenda of liberation. Where it is not, the text, because of
the frailty of the humans who composed it, must be challenged and, if need be, resisted as much as the system of
slavery it was purported to support. In this way the slaves
were perhaps the first biblical critics in America to read
so aggressively from "in front of the text" that they could
recognize the text for what it really was, the *words* first-
century human writers employed in their attempt to con-
vey the *Word* of the eternal God.

A Living Word: The New Testament Writers

The biblical authors themselves also looked at the biblical
words in the same way. The New Testament authors didn't
see the words of the Old Testament as the last word, for
they interpreted the Old Testament words time and time

again in light of their own contextual circumstances, in light of the circumstances of the churches to whom they were writing, and in light of who Jesus perpetually is. Psalm 2:7 is an example: "You are my son," the Psalmist proclaims for God; "today I have begotten you." Of course, in the Psalmist's own time this language was about the Davidic king who would be, at his enthronement, considered begotten of God. The word in that form, however, if it were to stay in that form, would be a dead word in a time when Davidic kingship itself no longer existed. But the Lordship of Jesus Christ *did* exist. And that is why, when New Testament writers from the Gospels to Revelation interpreted those words of the Psalmist, they interpreted them in light of Jesus and either his baptism or his crucifixion.[5]

Examples like this are legion. Perhaps one of the best things to do is to look at how the New Testament writers interpreted not only the Old Testament but also each other. Clearly, Matthew and Luke, who used Mark as a source for their own words, felt that the Spirit of God was still on the move, so that they could change Mark's words in ways that were applicable to their contexts and people and, indeed, change Mark's Gospel itself. So they added the birth narratives where there were none and resurrection stories that Mark did not himself deploy. And they adjusted stories in the text so that, for example, in the storm on the sea, Jesus' words about the disciples' complete lack of faith becomes in Matthew a less harsh word about their little faith that has the possibility of growth. Why? Because in Matthew's community the disciples played a more important role in the life of the community of faith, and it just wouldn't do for them to have appeared as ignorant in Matthew's telling of the story as they did in Mark's.

We might also consider Luke, who was writing to a Gentile audience and trying to call them to faith in Christ Jesus. Little wonder, then, that when he got to Mark's story about the Syrophoenician woman, where Jesus calls Gentiles "dogs," he decided to edit those words out of his word.

Then there's Paul. Given the shift in situation from Jesus' time to his, Paul felt the need to adjust even *Jesus'* words. Even Jesus' words! Actually, he did more than that. He took a leap and wrote new material because the context demanded it. At 1 Corinthians 7:10–15, Paul first cites Jesus by saying, "This is the Word of the Lord." He goes on to say how Jesus' words disallow divorce. But then he does something radical. He says, "To the rest I say—I and not the Lord," that if a situation arises that is different from the one Jesus envisioned, where a pagan is married to a believer and threatens to pull that believer from his or her faith, then it is perfectly permissible to let the pagan partner go his or her own way. This is a living word of authority from a man who believes he is in contact with the Spirit of Christ who is still living in his midst.

The New Testament and Homosexual Behavior: The Search for a Living Word

The New Testament's words on homosexual behavior are also clear. They are words of condemnation; I don't try to deny that. I don't think anyone should. But they are words out of a particular context. Our context is so significantly different that I don't think the words are any longer living, but are, rather, dead words if we try to read them without contextually understanding them today.

Paul was inspired by God's Word in a world where sexuality was understood in a radically different way from how it is understood today. In fact, homosexuality as we presently understand it wasn't a part of the early church's secular or religious vocabulary. No one talked in terms of a genetic predisposition or early social conditioning and learning, or a way of life, or a nurturing, caring partnership of two people. That's because such a concept did not exist. What existed instead was a first-century pagan, Jewish, and developing Christian understanding of which individual sex acts could or could not be seen as appropriate.

When we consider the surrounding cultural perspectives on the issue, we see that in this case Paul was very much speaking from and with his surrounding culture in an accommodating rather than a prophetic way. Philosophers of the day, such as Seneca and Dio Chrysostom, considered same-sex activity to be driven by dehumanizing lust. They recognized, of course, that lust was not just a problem for same-sex activity but that it plagued relationships between men and women as well. To them, because sexual activity driven by lust was dehumanizing in all cases and same-sex activity was always motivated by lust, it therefore always had to be avoided. Other philosophers, such as Plutarch, argued that love between a man and woman was natural. Sexual activity between people of the same gender was considered dehumanizing because it was unnatural. By "unnatural" they meant, of course, that it had nothing to do with procreation, the condoned purpose of sexual activity between men and women.

The two primary secular concerns with same-sex activity, then, were the unreasonable motivation of lust and the unnatural quality of the acts. As Victor Paul Furnish notes, "When we turn now to Paul's remarks about such conduct, it becomes apparent that he perceived it in essentially the same way."[6]

New Testament writers did, of course, have a different

starting point. For Paul, sexual activity between persons of the same sex was a direct result of idolatry, the human acceptance of false gods or a false understanding of their own relationship before the gods. Paul was thinking of individual, separate actions as God's punishment for idolatry. He was not thinking, nor was he prepared to think, in terms of relationship. He was thinking of what humans did and not what God had created, a person predisposed by reason of biology or social learning toward relationship with other persons of the same gender. For him the issue was one of controlling behavior, not running from or living out one's human identity.

In this kind of thinking, one's behavior was proper if it fit the intentions of creation, which pushed procreation, not sexual intimacy, and controlled not only the type but also the frequency of that intimacy. One performed such acts not as a way of sharing intimacy but of procreating the human species or checking the fires and flames of passion between men and women. The contemporary understanding of intimate homosexual union that often expresses itself physically and celebrates passion within a committed relationship was as alien to Paul as Paul knew the possibility of a believer marrying a pagan was alien to Jesus. So Paul did what others in his Greco-Roman context were doing: He tied his understanding of sexuality to an understanding of sex acts that were properly condoned only when done according to the natural order designed for procreation or as a remedy for the burning passions of lust that apparently threatened the eruption of human bonfires all over the ancient world.

There are times, though, when Paul breaks beyond the boundaries of social expectation in the ancient world and cracks through the status codes implied in creation. His work with the church at Galatia is a case in point. Here the Jewish-Gentile issue takes center stage. His letter opens with the immediate presumption of a grave crisis (1:6–9): Some people who have entered the community are teaching a radically different gospel. Paul's work of bringing together Jew and Gentile into the same community of faith is in jeopardy, at least in the manner that he had envisioned. His opponents in Galatia agree that Jews and Gentiles may worship together in one community of faith. They demand, however, that Gentiles earn the right to be included by observing major components of the Jewish Law, particularly the ritual components dealing with circumcision and dietary matters.

Paul, though, is already on written record, in his correspondences to Thessalonica (1 Thess. 2:12; 3:3; 4:7; 5:9, 24)[7] and Corinth (1 Cor. 2:2), arguing that inclusion into the people of God is based on God's election through the gospel of Christ, specifically the gospel that records Christ's death on the cross. It is God's action, through Christ, that determines one's inclusion into the people of God, not one's adherence to and compliance with the Jewish Law. This means, however, that if the Law is no longer the deciding factor, but God's act in Christ, then anyone and everyone who believed in that act could become a part of the people of God. It is this kind of radical thinking that provokes Paul when he makes his radical statement at Galatians 3:28:

> There is no longer Jew or Greek, there is no longer slave or free, there is no longer male and female; for all of you are one in Christ Jesus.

A community whose theology of justification by faith led to a social reality where slave and free, male and female, Jew and Gentile lived on an equal plane would have been radically countercultural indeed. Faith, then, has worked itself out in an incredibly liberating, boundary-breaking, countercultural way. As Wolfgang Schrage points out in his book on ethics in the New Testament, now, after Galatians 3:28, "In the one body of Christ, all secular categories are transcended, even distinctions inherent in the created order."[8]

This is a crucial point. Paul's understanding of God's actions in Christ lead him to the almost insane conclusion that even the categories that God established in the act of creation have now been superseded. *Even the biblical words of human creation are not the last words for human living.* The boundaries standardized for all time at the very beginning of time have been eschatologically smashed down in the act of Jesus' coming, death, and resurrection. Here is a place where Paul's Christ theology crashes hard up against his creation theology, shattering the territorial lines it imposed, redrawing the orders of separation it enacted, and, along the way, inaugurating the genesis of a very different kind of human social and ethical landscape.

The implications are staggering. In Paul's thought, God's doing is simultaneously the mandate for human living. The shattering of creation's boundaries that occurs with Jesus' death and resurrection is the gracious provocation of a new eschatological reality that enables human transgressions of the same kind. All people, regardless of gender, ethnicity, race, stature, or—dare I say it even though Paul does not—sexual preference, are equally acceptable in God's sight and therefore must be equally treated in human living.

What I'm suggesting, of course, is that contexuality is not only important when we compare Paul to our time but also it is important—indeed, imperative—when we compare Paul to the Paul of his own time. When the contextual base of his theology shifts, so does the emphasis in his ethics. When that theology operates from the radical thing that God has done through Christ Jesus, then boundaries break down and people rise up and are brought together. This is Paul's *living* word, the one that continues into our own time and gives us hope for the way in which all people who have been created as God has created them, just as they are, might be treated equally and accepted faithfully *together* in the one body of faith.

Living with the Living Word

We can't be faithful and we can't get to God's truth if the biblical words don't live for us like this. The gospel is not useful to us if we don't interpret like this. This is the way our human spirits hear God's voice today. We can follow the Paul who followed the trail of divine, living activity, and we can challenge the Paul who operated in his culture with words driven from a theology of creation that endorses slavery, devalues women, reveres every government, and appears to denounce gay and lesbian sexuality.

This is difficult, I know, because the words are biblical words, the words are in the canon, and we find it hard to challenge them no matter their context because every word is supposed to be the last word. That's why inclusive language is often so difficult for many people to accept when they read the Bible. The words, the pronouns *he*, *him*, and *his*, have become THE WORD. A faith mathematics of simple addition takes hold. All the words form an equation that equals faith. Just as, in mathematics, we need every number if the total sum in a simple addition problem is going to be correct, so every word must be equally authoritative if simple faith is going to add up. So the words *his* and *him* become just as important as the words *justification* and *cross*. Mess with either one and you're messing equally with the faith. So the words "slaves obey your masters" (Eph. 6:5; Col. 3:22) or "women be silent in church" (1 Cor. 14:34) must be equal to the words "Those who say, 'I love God,' and hate their brothers or sisters, are liars" (1 John 4:20). So the words "their women exchanged natural intercourse for unnatural, and in the same way also the men, giving up natural intercourse with women, were consumed with passion for one another" (Rom. 1:26–27) become as important as "There is no longer Jew or Greek, there is no longer slave or free, there is no longer male and female; for all of you are one in Christ Jesus" (Gal. 3:28). Every word, no matter how it's tied to its context, must be the last word, or faith itself is somehow challenged.

Such a perspective on the biblical words does a disservice to the power of the living Word to confront, challenge, and liberate us in the places where God's Holy Spirit of Christ meets us *today*. I know it's hard to think like this. It's hard to give up the simplicity of thinking that every word is the last word, no matter how tied it was to its own time and history. When I think of how hard it is, I remember that line from the Tom Hanks character, the team manager, in the movie *A League of Our Own*. When one of his players tells him that playing baseball is too hard, he responds to her, "It's baseball. It's supposed to be hard. If it weren't hard, then everyone would do it."

Christian faith, and the biblical interpretation that goes along with it, supports it, and directs it, is hard. Not everyone can do it; not everyone wants to do it. Many want the comfort of having someone just say forget about the contexts, forget about how the biblical writers were writing for their people in their time, forget about all that and just read all the words as the last word and do what they say, whatever they say. Even if I don't want to tell a slave to go back to his master; even if I don't want to tell a woman to sit down and keep quiet in church, and cover her head while she's at it; even if I don't want to tell someone politically oppressed to obey a government without protest when I think it's wrong; and even if I don't want to tell a gay or lesbian couple that they are idolatrous, lusting, unnatural sinners whom I'll love even though they have absolutely no business and no place in the kingdom of God, I'll do it anyway because it's easy. It's simple. And I long for a simple faith. I'll cry, but I won't do differently. I won't try to find a way to do differently because it's too hard.

It's supposed to be hard, stupid! Whoever would be my disciple must take up my hard cross and follow, follow daily, follow into tomorrow, where every word is a *living* word for people living where they are in their present and future, not in somebody else's past.

When you talk this way, say this kind of thing to new seminarians, you get fear. I've heard the words time and time again. "You're taking away my faith when you tell me all of this stuff about interpreting the words, understanding the words in light of our living, and not just taking all the words just as they are, no matter how tied they were to their first-century contexts. You're taking away my faith." And we listen, we struggle, and we wonder what to say as we tell them we'll try to help them rebuild their faith. When in truth, when they charge, "You're taking away my faith," we ought to respond, "No, this *is* your faith. Your *living* faith. I'm trying to give it back to you. This is how the first Christians did faith, aggressively using it to interpret, not just recite their traditions. The Spirit was alive, and the Word of God was on the move. You couldn't catch it, and you couldn't hold it so you'd be safe and secure. You had to move on dangerous ground with it."

Why? Because the biblical words are not the last Word. They are the *living* Word.

Notes

1. Quoted by Lee Cormie, "Revolutions in Reading the Bible," in *The Bible and the Politics of Exegesis*, 188. David Jobling, Peggy L. Day, Gerald T. Sheppard, eds. (Cleveland: Pilgrim Press, 1991).
2. Howard Thurman, *Jesus and the Disinherited* (Nashville: Abingdon Press, 1949), 30–31.
3. Vincent Harding, "Religion and Resistance among Antebellum Slaves, 1800–1860," in *African-American Religion: Interpretative Essays in History and Culture*, ed. Albert J. Raboteau and Timothy E. Fulap (New York and London: Routledge, 1997), 120.
4. Jacquelyn Grant, *White Women's Christ and Black Women's Jesus* (Atlanta: Scholar's Press, 1989), 212.
5. See Mark 1, Revelation 12.
6. Victor Paul Furnish, *The Moral Teaching of Paul* (Nashville: Abingdon, 1979), 67.
7. Frank J. Matera, *New Testament Ethics: The Legacies of Jesus and Paul* (Louisville, Ky.: Westminster John Knox Press, 1996), 123.
8. Wolfgang Schrage, *The Ethics of the New Testament*, trans. David E. Green (Philadelphia: Fortress Press, 1988), 223.